THE RABBIT WHO GOT AWAY

Nicola Austin
The Rabbit Who Got Away

Published by BooxAI

ISBN: 978-965-578-665-1

THE RABBIT WHO GOT AWAY

Nicola Austin

Acknowledgments

It is with deepest gratitude I would like to extend a big thank you to those who made this book possible.

Firstly, I want to thank God for giving me the wisdom and knowledge to write this book. With Him, all things are possible. I would also like to dedicate this book to my niece Kasi Fenelus and my nephew Kiyan Fenelus. I love you always and forever. To my husband, Andre Austin. My mom, Joy Johnson. My sister, Kadian Fenelus. My godsister, Jada Weekes. Goddaughter Kelis Edwards and godson Jacob Fong Hong, I love you and thank you for your support.

Once upon a time. There was a family that lived in the woods by a big lake.

The family consisted of Mom and Dad and two children.

The daughter's name was Kasi.

The son's name was Kiyan.

Mom and Dad bought the children a white rabbit they called him Snowball.

Snowball loved to eat carrots. Whenever Kasi and Kiyan visited Mima, they fed their pet rabbit his favorite meal.

One weekend, Mom and Dad took the kids to visit Mima's. They loved going to Grandma Mima's house. She lived in the suburbs and had a big backyard and a beautiful garden.

It was always fun visiting Grandma Mima's house.

But little did they know that something sad was going to happen. That weekend Kasi and Kiyan were in a rush to see Mima and forgot to lock Snowball's cage.

When the family arrived at Grandma Mima's house, they swam and played hide and seek.

After a long day of having fun, they ate dinner.

It was time to go home. They said their goodbyes to Grandma Mima. Mom and Dad gathered their stuff and drove home on the busy highway.

When they arrived home, Snowball's cage was empty. He was missing. Kasi and Kiyan frantically ran, "Mommy, Daddy Snowball is missing. We accidentally left his cage open when we went to visit Grandma Mima's house." Mom replied, "Don't worry honey, we will find Snowball."

Snowball the silly rabbit.

Snowball liked to play and have fun; sometimes, he liked to sneak off and explore his surroundings.

Snowball was hungry, and his cage was left open to his surprise. He then spotted an orange object. He thought it was a juicy carrot, but to his disappointment, it was his toy carrot.

So a Hippity Hoppity Snowball escaped right through the back door.

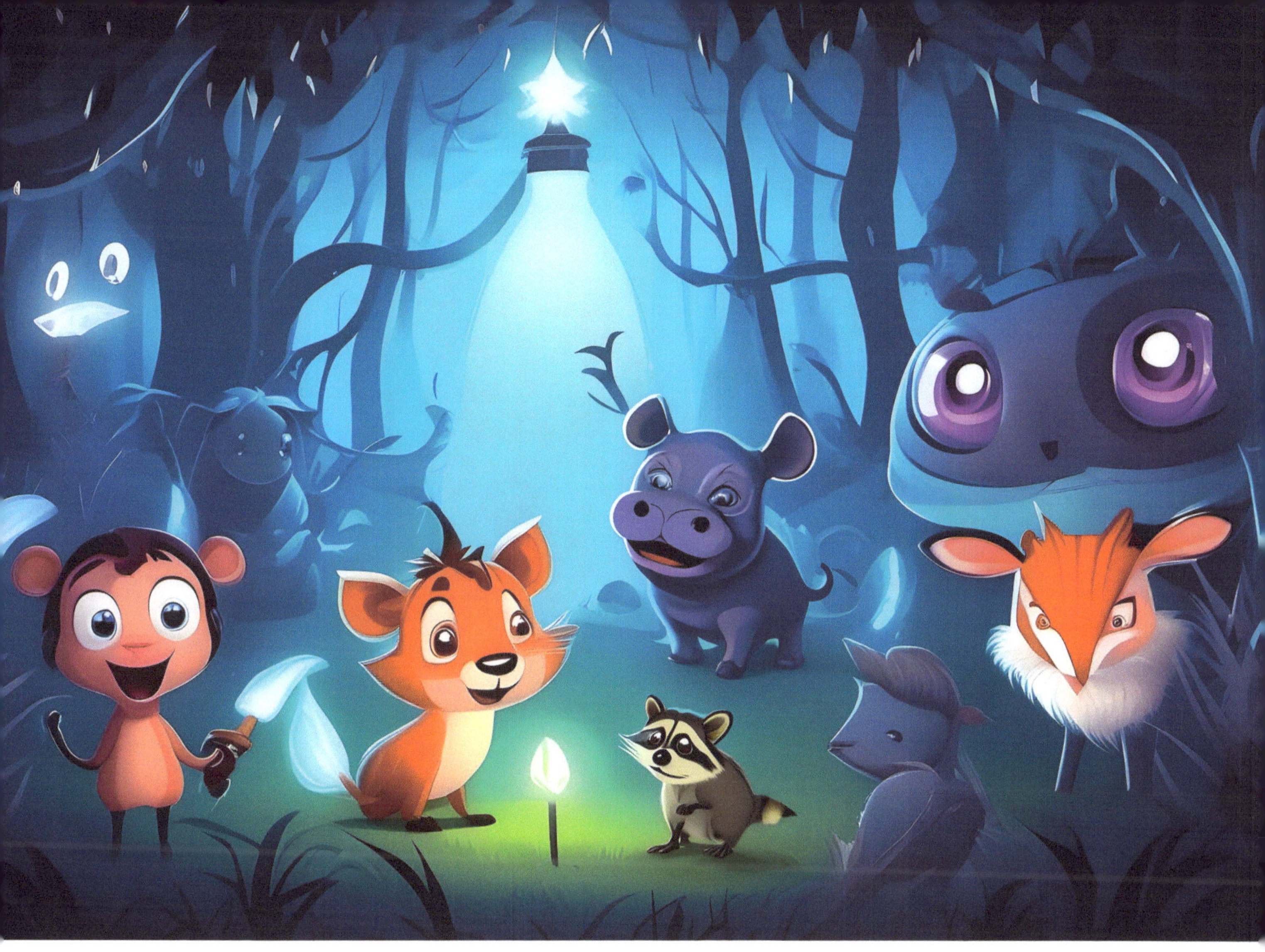

As the sun began to set, a nervous Kasi and Kiyan were scared for their beloved lost pet rabbit, Snowball. The children knew that other big and scary animals lived in the woods.

So Mom, Dad, Kasi, and Kiyan grabbed a flashlight and headed to the woods to search for Snowball.

Once the family entered the woods Kasi and Kiyan started to shout out and call Snowball in hopes that he would Hippity Hoppity out of the bushes.

Suddenly, the bushes in the flower bed started to rattle. Kasi and Kiyan made their way over, peeping and moving the tall shrubs out of the way. Kasi and Kiyan were startled when they noticed a hole. They turned their flashlights on and pointed it down to take a better look.

A spooked Snowball sat scared inside a deep hole he dug into and could not find his way out of.

"Mom and Dad, over here, we found Snowball. He looks like he's stuck inside this hole."

The family worked as a team, rescued Snowball, and brought him back home. The family was over the moon with excitement that they had found their beloved pet rabbit, Snowball. After Snowball was all cleaned up, the children put their pet rabbit in his cage and fed him his favorite juicy carrot.

Kasi and Kiyan were exhausted and were ready for bed. They took a nice warm bath and headed to bed. Mom and Dad came into the room and read their favorite bedtime story. Before Kasi and Kiyan fell asleep, Mom and Dad asked them what lesson they learned today.

They responded, "Mom, Dad, we will never leave the house again before checking Snowball's cage."